HAVING TWO HOMES

By
Holly Duhig

BookLife
PUBLISHING

©2018
BookLife Publishing
King's Lynn
Norfolk PE30 4LS

A catalogue record for this book is
available from the British Library.

ISBN: 978-1-78637-399-1

Written by:
Holly Duhig

Edited by:
Kirsty Holmes

Designed by:
Amy Li

HAVING TWO HOMES

Words that look like **this** can be found in the glossary on page 24.

What Is Separation?

Sometimes, parents live together, but other times, our parents live apart. Sometimes, parents who live together decide they don't want to live together anymore. This is called separation.

If people who are married want to live apart, they might get divorced. This means they will not be married anymore.

"When my mum and dad divorced, Dad went to live in a new house. Luckily it wasn't far away, so I could go and stay with him on weekends."

Amy – aged 7

Why Do People Separate?

Some people separate because they are finding it hard to get along. They might have lots of fights, or realise they **disagree** on lots of things.

Sometimes people decide they would be happier if they lived apart.

"My friend Maisy wanted to play football at break time and I didn't. We still like each other but we don't play together anymore."

Bella – aged 6

This might have happened to you. Have you ever fallen out with a friend at school because you had a disagreement or liked different things?

What Happens When Parents Divorce?

Getting divorced is quite complicated. Married people have to ask a **court** for a divorce. It can take a long time because lots of important decisions have to be made.

One of these decisions is where everyone is going to live. Even though your parents don't want to live together, they still want to take the best care of you.

"Mummy told me that when parents separate, their love grows into two of everything – two beds, two houses, two gardens!"

Noah – aged 6

Talking About Your Feelings

If your parents are separating, you might have lots of questions. This is OK. Let your parents know how you are feeling and they will be able to help you.

Family Counsellor

You can also talk to a **family counsellor**. Some counsellors are trained to help people whose families are changing or separating.

You Might Feel Sad

You might feel sad if your parents are separating. You might feel like you want to cry or you might want to stop doing the things you enjoy. It's OK to feel like this.

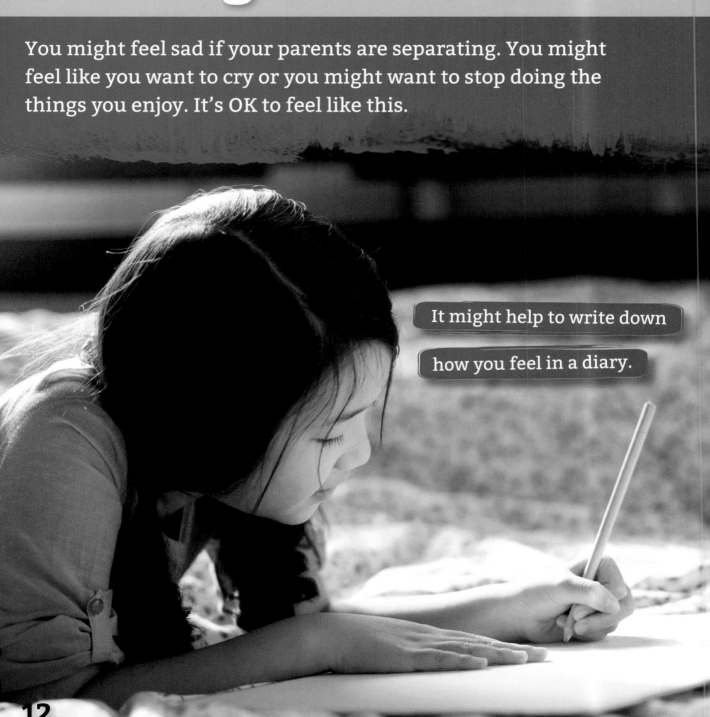

It might help to write down how you feel in a diary.

When parents separate, there might be lots of changes. This can be upsetting at first. However, soon these changes will start to feel normal.

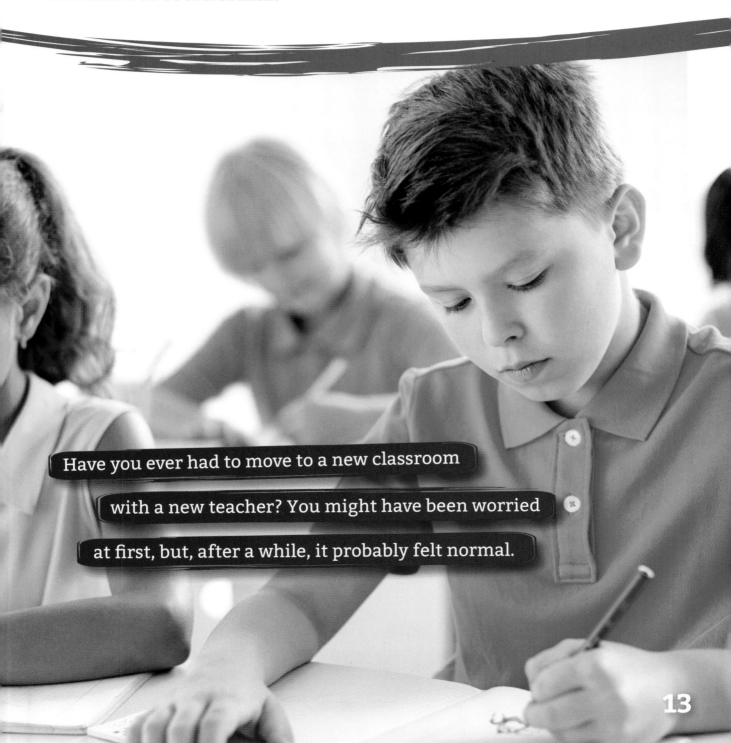

Have you ever had to move to a new classroom with a new teacher? You might have been worried at first, but, after a while, it probably felt normal.

You Might Feel Guilty

Lots of children worry that their parents have split up because of something they did. This is never the case. Separation is never anyone's fault.

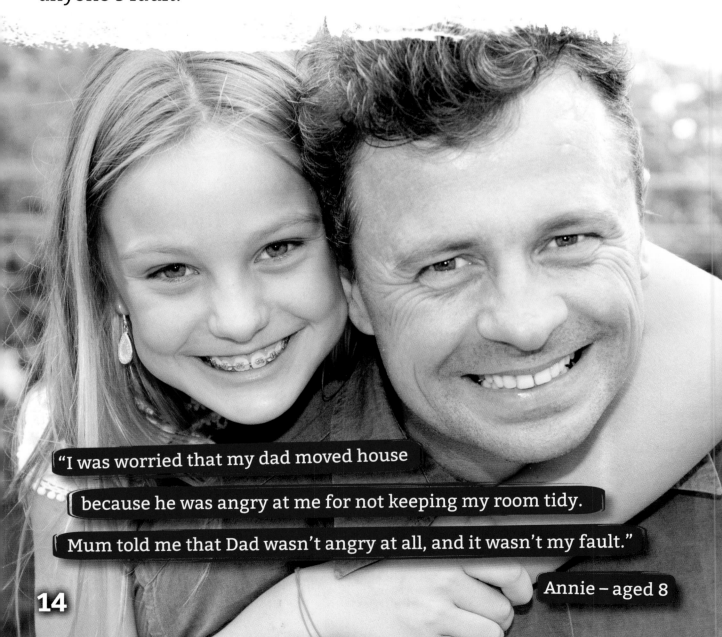

"I was worried that my dad moved house because he was angry at me for not keeping my room tidy. Mum told me that Dad wasn't angry at all, and it wasn't my fault."

Annie – aged 8

Some children live at one parent's house on weekdays, if it's closer to their school.

You might spend more time at one parent's house than the other. There's no need to feel guilty about this. This usually happens because it's more **practical**.

You Might Feel Angry

When people separate, they don't get back together. This might make you feel angry or frustrated. Tell your parents how you feel and they can help you.

"My friend's parents are still together. This made me feel jealous and cross. My parents told me there's no need to feel jealous because we are still a family who love each other very much."

Xavier – aged 7

It's normal to feel angry when parents divorce. You might want to scream and shout. However, it is important not to shout at other people, or hurt their feelings.

Playing a sport can help you to calm down when you're angry.

You Might Feel Worried

When people divorce, lots of things can change. This might make you feel worried. However, change can often be a good thing.

"At my mum's house I play with my friend, Artem.

At my dad's I play with my new neighbour, Jake."

Maria – aged 7

Lots of things change, but parents always love their children
no matter what.

Having Two Homes

There are lots of **advantages** to having two different homes. You might have two bedrooms which you can **decorate** differently.

"My mum and dad don't live together anymore, but I don't mind. I have two bedrooms and two toy boxes, and on my birthday, I get two cakes!"

Cleo – aged 6

One of your parents might live in the countryside where you can go for lots of walks. The other might live in a town where you can go shopping.

Most parents who divorce still live close together.

This is because it's more practical.

Stepfamilies

There are lots of different types of family. Sometimes mums and dads meet new partners and start new families. This might feel like a big change at first.

"I have two stepsisters. They are really nice to me and they let me share their toys."

Jason – aged 7

Your parent's new partner might have children of their own. They might become your **step-siblings**.

GLOSSARY

advantages	to be in a better position than someone else
court	a place where legal decisions can be made
decorate	to add something to an object or room to make it look better
disagree	a difference of opinion
family counsellor	a person whose job it is to listen and give advice to families
practical	likely to work well with little difficulty
step-siblings	the sons and daughters of your parent's new partner

INDEX